THE ABC'S TO EFFECTIVE SUBSTITUTE TEACHING

DR. YVONNE HENDERSON

Copyright © 2020

Transitions Publishing

P.O. Box 1361

Missouri City, TX 77489-1361

All rights reserved. No part of this book may be reproduced or transmitted in any form or by any means without written permission from the author.

TABLE OF CONTENTS

A   Page 6

B   Page 9

C   Page 11

D   Page 14

E   Page 17

F   Page 19

G   Page 22

H   Page 25

I   Page 28

J   Page 31

K   Page 33

L   Page 36

M   Page 39

N   Page 42

O   Page 45

P   Page 48

Q   Page   51

R   Page   54

S   Page   57

T   Page   59

U   Page   61

V   Page   64

W   Page   67

X   Page   70

Y   Page   72

Z   Page   75

Affirmation Page 78

Sub Notes 79

PREFACE

This guide was written to help those who would so dare to venture out into the classroom from another path to become a substitute teacher. My hope is this will help you transition from one career to another.

DEDICATION

This guide is dedicated to every man and woman who would dare step foot in our shoes, if only for a moment to help our students continue their educational journey. It may at times feel like a thankless job, but there is a student out there who needs you, so dust yourself off relearn your ABC's and go change a life.

Dr. Yvonne Henderson

Ascertain /Assert

Use your ability to ascertain the situation and come up with a plan to command the room and assert your values to defuse any obstacle.

Having a Sargant from the military as my dad gave me the background and ability to know how to command a room with both silence and my words.

Commanding a room does not always require you to be the one doing all the talking.

The first time I subbed in a middle school I had to do this a little different than I did with the elementary age students. As the students entered, I greeted them and asked them to take a set. Once everyone was seated, I stood quietly at the entrance of the room to ascertain the situation. As the students noticed they began telling their classmates' to be quiet and face forward. Within a matter of minutes all the students were facing me. I did not have to say anything, I asserted what I had. My presence was different, my demeanor was different, and it commanded their attention in a different way.

I thanked them for their attention and introduced myself. I then gave them guidelines needed to the complete the work that was left by their teacher and where to submit it at the end of the class period.

You must remember that you are the adult and you must assert your authority to ensure things run smoothly. You do not have to be nasty or demanding because that will just create a power struggle, that is not how you want to enter or try and run the class because you will have that one student that is going to try you. That is a chapter in another book.

B

Believe/Benefits

Believe in yourself and what you are capable of in the classroom for the students. What are the benefits that you bring to the classroom?

Believe in yourself. Why are you doing this? You became a substitute teacher because you believed you could make a difference. You believed you had something to offer. You believed you could do this. So, what has changed? Oh, you had a kid or two swear at you, so now you do not think you are cut out for this. Wrong, you are, they are lashing out because kids have a hard time dealing with change. Do not you change on them too. Be the change they need that will push them to succeed. Let them know that even though things change they do not have to fall apart. Make them believe you are there for them.

You are there for a reason, what can they benefit from you. Share some things with them to let them know you understand them and are there for them. What are some things you bring to the classroom that others may find beneficial to use in other classrooms?

C

Caring/Contributing

Show the students you genuinely care about their education. Contribute to the students. Give them some tips on how to complete an assignment with excellence.

Have you heard the phrase; Caring is sharing. Well. If you care about something you show it. When you walk into a classroom the students are hoping to get a substitute teacher that will care. Go in with an attitude that shows you care. Use positive comments when speaking to the students. My mom used to say, "If you don't have anything nice to say, don't say anything at all." At the end of the day we must remember they are kids.

What do you contribute to the students and school you are working for? What do you have that someone else does not have? Why should they ask you back? Do not just sit and do nothing, contribute to the learning experience.

Engage with the students by looking over the lesson, reading to see what they need to do so you will be able to answer questions they may have about the lesson. You could do the assignment with them or read any necessary passages to be able to give accurate help in facilitating their learning process. This would be a great way to show you care by contributing to the learning process. Contributing also means with your time. If you are in a classroom, engage with the students contribute to what they are learning by giving examples, or telling stories to grab their attention about a given story.

D

Dedication/Devote

Have dedication with every assignment. Come prepared to teach and not sit and read the newspaper or surf your social media accounts. Devote your time to the students while you are there, give them your undivided attention.

Having dedication to what you are doing could be difficult depending on the type of class you get. I know it is hard to work with hard to serve kids, but when you realize they are the ones who need you most you begin to devote your time to them and develop a real awareness to what is needed it allows you to become more dedicated. You will begin to research ways to reach the students. You will want to return to try and instill more in them. To be a part of their learning process begins to drive you and what you do. You cannot put a price on dedication or devotion.

Being devoted to something means that you care about it. You cannot be devoted to something and not care about it. If you have a job that you do on a consistent basis then nine times out of ten you are devoted to it. When you become a substitute teacher if you are not devoted to it you will find yourself frustrated and not believing in yourself the, students, or what you do. In the end being devoted and dedicated will cause you to make some changes in the way you operate.

E

Effort/Effective

Always give your best effort in any assignment. Always give yourself time, arrive early enough to look over the lesson.

Previewing lessons will help you be more effective in carrying out the teachers plans.

When you accept an assignment try to put some effort into your work. Most substitutes just go in, sit back, and collect a paycheck. Then the worse thing one could do is, talk about how lazy the students are and the misbehavior your encounter. When you go in with a different mindset to effect change and put forth an effort to teach things may go better. I said may, all students re different, so, do like I do, prepare for the worse scenario and work hoping for the best.

There may even be times when you enter a room and the students put forth an effort to keep with teachers' expectations and do their work. Every experience will bring different challenges and results. As the substitute teacher it is your job to keep procedures and expectations as normal as possible in the teacher's absence.

F

Fear/Fair/Feelings

In your instructions and management ensure you are being fair to all students. Let students know you have feelings and you are not a robot. Show no fear when you are in an unfamiliar situation.

Walking into an established class could be a little intimidating for a substitute teacher. Conquering your fear will allow you to carry out your duties in an effective manner. If you ever walk into a classroom fearful the students will sense that and it may be the roughest day of your career. Students sense fear, so you must be in control and command the room.

When dealing with students make sure all your decisions and consequences are fair and consistent. Take the students feelings into consideration when dealing with them. Some educator may not agree with this, but you must realize you do not know the students and when given the opportunity they could probably help you with procedures. When you go into a classroom with good intentions and feelings, you can accomplish so much mor, when students feel you are truly there to support them. Remember, they have feelings just like you, so do not go in throwing your weight around demanding things. To get respect you must give respect.

G

Good/Goodies

Acknowledge students who are being good. Leave a positive note for the teacher letting them know who was good that day. Try and have goodies on hand to pass out for good behavior and incentives to keep students engaged.

Good things come to those who wait. You may feel like you are unappreciated and misunderstood, well the students feel the same way. In waiting that word means "hope," having a hope that things will get better and some good will take place. Remember students are hoping that they get a good substitute teacher when their regular teacher is absent. We need to stop thinking that everything is about us. The students are affected by all of this as well.

Go into the situation knowing that all students have a potential to be good and do good. You may not see this the first time you substitute in a classroom or district but do know that students just want to make sure they have someone working with them that really wants them to do good. I am not asking you to try and change the world, but we can change one student at a time.

I like to reward students with goodies (treats). This is usually done when students are on point in class, when they have assisted me, or in the lesson in any way. When students feel valued, they work better. Things can be lightened a little to get results. Even the students who act up will get in line for a treat. They may say they do not care, or they don't want any, but they really do. They only say that because they do care. Know the best thing is to give them a treat at some point because they will eventually comply with what you ask them to do.

Help/Handle

Find out who need to contact if you need help. Do not waist a lot of time trying to figure things out when you are new to the system. Handle everyone with dignity and care. You do not want students to feel as though they are not important.

When you enter a room, understand that you are a guest and you do not know everything. You may get the best help ever from one of the students. Most teachers will leave you a couple of names of those students that will be helpful to you. If they do not, trust me you will have a student to come to you and help you with what you need to do and assist you with routines. Also find out what teachers or administrators you may call on if you need assistance. Usually, you could count on the teachers next to you to help you if you needed it. Or there may be specific team members that they will direct you to for assistance.

During your assignment be sure to handle all incidents in a professional manner. You should always make sure you try and handle each situation in the same manner for consistency. Students will accuse you of being racist and all other kinds of things when you treat them differently. So, make sure you are incredibly careful how you handle the students. Nowadays students will provoke you to get a rise out of you to have an opportunity to record you and then you could potentially be on the News, YouTube, or some other social media platform. Always handle yourself appropriately to protect yourself and your career. You also want to make sure you know how to handle the adults you are going to be working with. The other teachers may not give you the respect you deserve, or you feel you deserve, so just make sure you do not mishandle them when they come at you in a not so nice way.

I

Integrity/Influence

Use integrity when you are in charge. Do not do or say anything in the class you are not willing or able to repeat in-front of the parents or administrator. Your influence makes a difference whether you know it or not.

Sometimes we think we can do whatever we want behind closed doors with the students, however, that is the most crucial time. Your integrity is at stake. How do you act when people are not watching? Well, the students are watching, and they are the ones that count the most. Just because an administrator is not in the room does not give you a license to be nasty or disrespectful to the students. We owe it to ourselves to go into a classroom and be the best self we can be. We want to make sure we leave a good first impression. Hell, second and third expression, if we get the opportunity to return to a room or building.

You should be a positive influence for the students you are working with. Being in that room at that time has set you up to make a difference in at least one life.

Some may not like you, but always be true to who you are. How you carry yourself will not just resonate with the students, but they will in turn tell some other adult about you and how you were in their class. Use every opportunity as a chance to invoke change as an influencer. We should be building up not tearing down.

J

Jeopardize/Join

When you take an assignment, do not do anything to jeopardize you getting a call back. Join in, become a part of the staff not an outcast.

Whatever you do make sure you do not do anything to jeopardize your ability to return to that school or district. The wrong thing said to the wrong child, or adult could cause you a job. Even when we may not like something or we disagree with it, we do not have to always vice our opinion. Remember you are a guest at that school, and you do not want to jeopardize not being able to return.

I can remember situations that I did not think were good, but because I choose to just follow what I was asked to I was able to secure other assignments even when the situations were bad, administrators would thank me for keeping my cool and handling the situation when students were not respectable and parents would complain. You must know which battles are worth fighting and which ones are not.

Keep/Knowledge

Keep cool in every situation. Be knowledgeable about your surroundings and keep track of your assignments, they may become potential references.

Several things come to mind when I say keep. Keep your cool, keep going, keep your seat, keep your opinions to yourself, keep order in your class. This list could go on and on about the things we need to keep doing when we take on the responsibility of being a substitute teacher. You may not think these things matter but having self-control and keeping your composure when a student or adult rubs you the wrong way is especially important. Keep track of your assignments because they could become potential references. You may have to bite your tongue. You may wonder what I mean when I say keep your seat. Well, I remember a time where a student wanted to come at me and to refrain from retaliating I had to remain seated, because I knew if I gotten out of my seat things would have escalated because the student would have gone into fight mode. Keeping the respect, I had gained from students by not engaging in the disrespectful behavior allowed the other students to see I was being real with them. In most times the students would call out the disrespectful students and make them sit down, especially if they liked me, they would not let anyone disrespect me, so I did not have to fight for myself.

I cannot tell you how many videos or stories I have seen or heard about a substitute teacher who lost it in a classroom and was arrested and lost their job.

You may not know everything but have enough knowledge to know when to stand down and when to stand up. Know your surroundings, know your students, know the district. Being knowledgeable about these things could keep you out of a lot of trouble.

L

Lasting/Love/Limitations

Leave a lasting impression on students, staff, and administration. Love what you do and show it. Know your limitations.

Remember first impressions make a lasting impression. They can be both good and bad. In having a good lasting impression, it may cause you to be asked back on another assignment or recommended for other assignments. I can remember having to get a pocket calendar to take with me because when I would finish an assignment, they would always ask me my availability before I left the building. I had assignments book months in advance, and I was always asked back to a school or district on multiple occasions.

A bad lasting impression could end up with you not only returning to the school, but you may not be asked to return the district depending on what happened. This happened to me when I was given a letter not to return for the following year at Winter break, it was like a riff letter that teachers receive. As a result, I applied for unemployed because I had been let go. This district did not take it so well, because I won the unemployment case and they had to pay me unemployment, but then asked me not to come back to their district when the school year resumed. It was okay because I had three other districts that I was working with.

This could have been a problem had I not known my limitations. I did not feel I did anything I did not have a right to do. I was not limited by the districts I worked for. I could work for as many districts as I pleased, so therefore, I did not have any limitations on myself about acquiring work.

Memorable/Money

What will they remember you for?

Do not let money dictate the assignments you accept. You cannot put a price on helping students.

How will you be remembered by the students and the staff? Do you want to be remembered? I have had students see me in the grocery store and remember me from being in their classroom. It is a good feeling to have someone notice you outside of what you do, because of what you did. Let me break that down. If you are in a classroom working with students and when you leave, they do not remember you, there is a problem. If they remember you because you were mean and nasty, ore hard on them, at least they remembered you. But if you leave and they do not remember you at all, Whoa. You want to be remembered for something.

Know the money piece. If you went into the field of education with the mindset that you were going to make a whole lot of money, you are in the wrong profession. You may be aware the those higher up in education are getting paid, but a teacher, no and not a substitute teacher. You must be in education because you love kids, you love teacher, or you just flat out care about the learning process for all. I did not become a teacher for the money, even though I have been able to receive a nice chunk of change, but that is not the point. Nowadays you are paid according to your years of service, not your degrees. I have enough expertise to do just about anything I put my mind to, but I love teaching, I love seeing the lightbulb come on in students.

Nothing/Novice

Nothing is better than the feeling you get when you help a student achieve. Know that every class is going to be a new experience, therefore you are a novice in that classroom.

Just like any other job, you want to be able to bring something to the table. As a substitute, if you have never taught before, there is still an expertise that you bring. So, you do not have to feel like you have nothing to offer. Going into a class for the first time, you cannot go in empty handed with nothing. You could bring in a story to tell the students about your experience and how you became a substitute teacher. Students love to hear stories, so utilize everything you have. You must have something planned just in case the teacher did not get a chance to leave work, or the students run out of work. Either scenario is possible. If possible, you do not want to go into a classroom without having any type of backup plan

This may be your first time as a substitute, a novice so to speak, and you are not sure what to do. This is different from substituting in a grade or subject area for the first time. This is your very first time substituting at all. You could research the grade level you are going to and the type of assignments that would be appropriate for that grade. This could also give you some brownie points with the teacher to the point they want to request you again, or the principal sees you to be an asset.

Remember nothing is impossible when you put your mind to it.

Overdo/Opportunity/Overcome

Sometimes you must overdo it in the classroom. This will make room for opportunities. It will also allow you to overcome obstacle.

Most times in preparing for an assignment I would have to overdo it.

Being over prepared is better than being underprepared. When I was in college, we had to keep an expandable file folder with assignments for every subject for every grade. This was to help us be prepared for student teaching. It was such a good idea I kept doing it after graduation. Being prepared will help you win the students as well. Hard to believe, well contrary to what you heard or learned, students love to be engaged. Do not allow yourself to be overcome with fear and anxiety, you got this. You are well on your way to be a great substitute teacher.

Opportunities will present themselves when you go that extra mile. You can always find an opportunity in the classroom, to either help the students or the teacher in some way. Students love when you take opportunities to get to know them and not judge them or treat them a certain way because everyone has. Take opportunities to get to know the students even if you are only there for one day, especially in elementary schools because you have the students for most of the time. It may be a little harder in secondary because you switch classes every 40 to 50 minutes but do the best you can.

All of these will set you up to overcome any fear or anxiety you may have had. Overcoming possible obstacles will allow for success, especially, if you create your own way of handling things without call on the office for assistance, it will show you know how to manage your classroom.

P

Preparation/Positive/ Purpose

Always be prepared for your assignment whenever possible. Give thought to the subject you will be teaching. Prepare something extra. Go into every assignment with a positive attitude.

Preparation is everything. When you can walk into a room prepared, it shows the teacher, students', and administration that you want to be there. There is nothing I hate worse than a substitute who comes in unprepared. For that matter, I do not like entering a room where the students are not prepared. When students do not have what they need it creates distractions. The substitute does not want to go through the teacher's belongings trying to find supplies for the students. Believe me you do not want to open that can of worms. God forbid something comes up missing, because the first person that will be blamed is the substitute teacher. Trust me all the students are going to say you were going through the desk. I am telling you this from experience. I had to meet with the teacher and principal because I was accused of taking something out of a teacher's desk. It was later found, but it was still an uncomfortable position to be.

Even in the face of adversity remain positive. Things only get worse when you approach them from a negative standpoint. You have a better chance at being heard when you remain calm and positive.

Know your purpose, do not do anything that will jeopardize your purpose for being there. You are there to teach the students, make sure they continue their academic education in the absence of their teacher. You never want to lose sight of your purpose, when you do your work ethics will be compromised and you will not put your best foot forward, it will just become another job when you lose your purpose.

Quit/Quality

Quitting is not an option. Once you accept an assignment fulfill it to the best of your ability. Giving your best means giving your best quality of work.

Always realize quitting is not an option. Students have a hard time dealing with change. When substitutes come in for long term assignments it is always good to complete the assignment no matter what is going on in the classroom. Please do not quit or give up on the students they need you more than you need them.

Quality is the key, when you take over a classroom bring your best self, your "A" game. Make sure you enter the class with quality lessons and expectations for every student. The quality you get is based on the quality you put in. Quality is better than quantity. What good is it for all the students to turn in their assignments when it is completed incorrectly, and it will need to be done over. Finish fast, finish last.

Quality could also be quality control; how do you control the environment in which you are teaching. Are you able to keep the students on task, or are they running amuck in your classroom? Administrators love to have substitute teachers who can keep order in the classroom. It makes their job a lot easier when they do not have to come into your classroom every 15 minutes to deal with discipline.

Rest/Reflect

Make sure you get enough rest before reporting for an assignment. Proper rest helps you stay alert. Always reflect on your own performance after a completed assignment.

Over the years I have realized that making sure I am rested before entering a classroom makes the world of difference in how things will transpire. You may ask yourself, "What does how much sleep I get have to do with me teaching?" I am glad you asked. Several things could happen. If you do not get enough sleep, you oversleep and be late for an assignment. Not a good impression ever. If you do not get enough sleep you could report with a bad attitude and take it out on the students, or other staff members. Not getting enough sleep could cause you not to be alert and at your full capacity and something could break out in the class that you do not react to immediately and that could cause a whole other problem.

At the end of each assignment I would journal how my day went, good or bad. I would reflect on things I did well and things I could improve on for the next assignment. Doing this allows you to document your own growth pattern and to see what areas you have improved in and what areas you still need to work on. Self-reflection can sometimes be better, because most people are harder critics on themselves than others could ever be, so it causes you to tell yourself the truth about where you are.

S

Stable/Secure

Provide a stable and secure learning environment for the students in the teacher's absence. This will also secure future appointments for you.

So many times, students can feel out of sorts when their regular teacher is absent, so it is your responsibility to ensure they maintain a stable environment to learn in.

This may prove difficult at times, because students will put up a resistance for the substitute, but they still need to be reassured that their leaning will not suffer.

Once you've done this then it will be easy to not only secure their feelings, and hope in their future, but you will be able to secure a place in their hearts to know you actually care about their well-being. At that point they are also looking for you to keep them secure in their surroundings making sure they continue to feel safe while at school.

T

Teach/Trust

You are there to teach in the teacher's absence. Being able to build a level of trust in a short amount of time will help you go far in this profession. Students will work for people they trust.

One of the hardest things you will problem every have to do. Learn how to teach to students who do not know you and are not going to be willing to work for you. This is where you separate the weak from the strong. This is where the real test happens, can you teach in a hostile environment? These students are not going to take it light on you. They do not want you there and they will do everything in their power to let you know you are not wanted. This is when you dig into your bag of tricks and pull out some strategies to help you win them over. Find that one student that seems to be in control, befriend them and the rest of the class will follow suit. Now do not be surprised when that student may be the one who is giving the most problems. Once you have gained their trust, or at least one students trust, it will be easier for you to teach.

U

Useful/Understand

Do not just show up, be useful while you are there. Try and understand how the student is feeling with the change that has just happened.

When you enter a classroom remember that you are there to fill in for the teacher, but you also make to make sure you are useful. Utilize all your skills to ensure the students get the best they can get out of you for the day. Research shows that several substitute teachers go into classrooms and just sit at the desk drinking their coffee and reading the newspaper. Well know it is surfing social media or texting. This is a job not a vacation and it should be treated as such. Too often substitute teachers feel they are in the room to make sure a body is there with the students. This is not the case. In order to be useful, you must understand why you are there.

You need to understand your place and your position and how important you are in that moment. You are not there to babysit. You are not there to be a monitor or proctor. Your job is continuing the stream of education that they would receive if their teacher was still there. You play an important role in the lives of the students. They need you to survive just as much as you need them. So, take the time to understand your role as a substitute teacher, and play out your part like a champ.

V

Victory/Villain

How you enter a classroom will determine you having victory with the students or becoming a villain to the students. Celebrate the victories to keep from becoming the villain.

You have heard the phrase, "Your attitude determines your altitude." Well, it serves the same when you walk into a classroom. If you walk in defeated, you will be defeated. If you walk in thinking you can not handle it, you will not be able to handle it. If you walk in with a bad attitude, bad attitude is what you will get. So, walk in victorious and victory will be your reward. God in with the mindset that you are going to do well, and you will. Go in thinking this is going to be a great day and it will be. You determine your victory, so walk into it.

When you walk in try to keep the atmosphere as normal as possible. Try not to make too many changes from what the students are used to, or you will immediately create some enemies. If you want to become the villain, change up the way they do things and see what happens. It may be okay to change some things, but you may want to ask the students how they feel about it first. Like I said, they are not too fond of change, so be careful. You can tell if students like your or villainize you by the way they respond to you, or by the way they stick up for you when other students try to act out. Once you have gotten on their good side, there is nothing they will not do for you.

Win/Win

Being the outsider learn to create a win/win situation for everyone involved, you, the students, the absent teacher, and the school. When students continue to learn with you in the classroom it is a win/win.

Being the newcomer on the scene does not make life easy, so to make sure that you have a win/win situation try to make sure you follow the plans left by the teacher. Teachers love when you follow there plans and continue where they left off. It also makes is easy for the students to not feel out of sorts, because everything is picking up where it left off. Some teachers may choose to leave a lesson separate from what they have been teaching depending on how long they will be out and how detailed the lesson may need to be, it could just be easier for the teacher to leave a lesson that is a filler. Whatever the case may be just make sure you follow the teachers instructions and inform the students of what is going to happen so they may prepare themselves, especially, if it is different from what they have been learning. Students do not like surprises, so please advise them as to what is going on as much as possible.

You should always give yourself time before the school day starts to go over the lesson, locate materials you may need and to familiarize yourself with the classroom and procedures. This will give you a winning edge before you must encounter the students.

X

Xerox

Create a folder with xeroed copies of work for every subject at the grade levels you work with that can be used at any time in the classroom.

We talked about being prepared earlier with the expandable folder. Well, this is what you need to do. Xerox copies of things to do before you get there. You may also be allowed to use the copy machine to make copies, you just need to ask the office staff. You never know how many students you will have so it is just about impossible for you to have enough copies xeroxed for all the students for the whole day. Provided you get a chance to make copies, make sure you leave yourself with enough copies or a copy to put back in your folder.

Y

Yesterday/Yearn

You cannot worry about what happened yesterday, that is in the past now. Look to tomorrow and yearn for a better understanding of your craft and how you can improve.

You can not cry over spilled milk. I have heard that quit a bit in my life. Even though you may not be able to change what happened on yesterday, you can learn from it and try not to do it again. You will have a lot of yesterday's and just as many tomorrows. So do not cry over spilled milk, clean it up and move on.

Your mistakes from yesterday should propel you into your tomorrow with a yearning for more. Making mistakes and not learning from them will only hurt you. Every school, every class, and every student you encounter is going to be different. You are not going to be able to do the same thing the same way every time you substitute. I tell my students all the time, "Doing the same thing, the same way, everyday and expecting a different result, is the definition of crazy." At least that is my definition, not the one you will find in the dictionary.

Understand that some things you do may have to change. If you have the same students all day, you may be able to get away with doing things the same way all day. However, when you go to that school where they change classes every period, you are going to have to do things different every class period.

Z

Zoo/Zero

You many feel like you have just walked into a zoo but go forth with a zero tolerance. Set the tone for how you plan to run the class the first time a problem arises.

Contrary to popular belief, you did not enter a zoo, yeah I am sure sometimes it may see like you have entered a zoo by the way the students act, but I assure you, you are not at the zoo. Students will act according to how you treat them, if you treat them like low life, low class citizens they will act like low life, low class citizens. Hold students to a higher standard. When you go into a classroom treat it like it is ground zero, go in and set the tone for how you want to run the classroom.

No, I am not telling you not to follow the teachers plans and expectations, but I am saying you should go in and make it your own. You are not their regular teacher and you do not have the rapport set up to do things as they do. You must remember that you need to assess, ascertain, and command the situation. Starting with a strong statement like having a zero tolerance will establish with students that you mean business and you are not there to play with them. They still need to know they have someone capable to keep order and to make sure their learning continues. You must be able to take charge before students realize you are a novice and try to run over you.

AFFIRMATION

After 20 + years of teaching I have found these things work for me in the classroom. I started out as a substitute teacher and this would have been helpful tips for me. A few of these things I learned while completing my practicums and student teaching, unfortunately, there are no classes for people who want to be substitute teachers or guest teachers as they are so affectionately called now. I plan to change that.

For more content, trainings and events contact me at drhenderson77@gmail.com

Sub Notes

Sub Notes

Sub Notes

www.ingramcontent.com/pod-product-compliance
Lightning Source LLC
Chambersburg PA
CBHW052113070526
44584CB00017B/2463